Computer Come-Froms:
The Roots of Real-Time

Where did computers come from?
What are the roots of real-time
computing?
This book is dedicated to turning
sand into silicon micro-processing
chips. They make possible the
positive in human potential.

This book is written in "Mosaic Style." The brief words - like puzzle pieces - fit together to make a complete picture of computers.

Table of Contents

Count with Beads and Boards

Long ago, people invented numbers to count what they were trading like cows or baskets of wheat. Next, tools like the abacus were invented to keep track of buying and selling and business profits.

2

Later, shop keepers used "counting boards" to tally customer bills. The word, 'counter' still means the space between clerk and customer.

Did you know that Roman Numbers can't do math directly? The answer was figured out using Counting Boards which was then written in Roman Numbers.

Our numbers today are called Indo-Arabic. They were invented in India, learned by Arab Traders who taught them to Europeans who brought them to America.

Sense of the Census

US Law requires that every ten years all Americans be counted and data collected. This was easy when the country was small. When it was nearly time for the 1890 Census, the 1880 data was still uncounted. The government offered a prize to anyone who could solve the problem of counting people. Herman Hollerith won.

He used punch cards to record answers to the census questions. Holes represented how many people, where they lived and how much they made. The punch cards were processed by machines. Pins poked through holes in the cards. They moved dials to record the data. It was a huge success.

6

Punch Cards represent data as 'holes or no holes'. Herman's company became International Business Machines, IBM. They used punch card computing machines for the next 80 plus years.

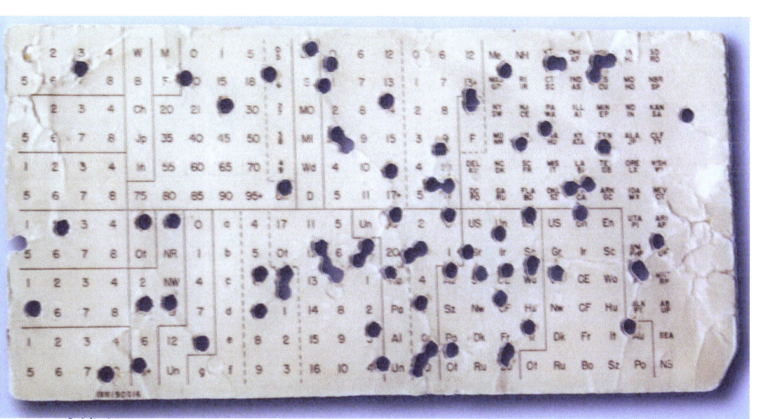

Public Domain

8

Codes and Crackers

In the 1920's, Enigma was invented so banks could send encrypted messages. No one bought the machines until the 1930's. Hitler and the Nazi's used Enigma and Lorenz machines to send secret military messages.

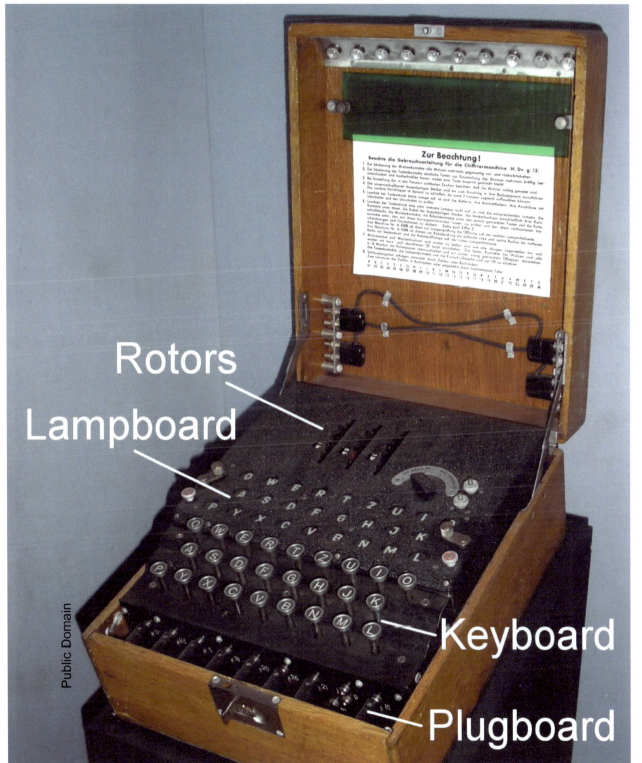

Rotors

Lampboard

Keyboard

Plugboard

10

In World War II, the British built a "computer" called "Colossus" to crack the Nazi's code. It worked! It is estimated this shortened the war by two years.

12

Aims of ENIAC

Also in World War II, the US Army had a problem aiming artillery accurately. They built a computer called ENIAC to calculate how to better aim the guns in different environments like the desert. ENIAC had 18,000 vacuum tubes.

Public Domain

It is estimated that during the decade ENIAC was in operation, it made more calculations than all humans had done up to that point in time.

14

On or Off Tubes

Each vacuum tube is a bit of data. Electricity flows through logic gates that switch tubes on or off. This turns raw data into information. Vacuum tubes were also used in radios and radars. Vacuum tubes burn out often and have to be changed like light bulbs.

16

No Patents on Computers

There were multiple lawsuits where many people claimed to have invented the computer. The courts ruled that no one person owned the computer. This made it easier to improve the computing machines.

18

Phone Line Links

Since the telephone was invented in the 1870's, wires were routed around the world to connect people in different cities and countries. Key to this, is switchboard computers that direct the calls. Bell AT&T's computers used vacuum tubes to switch the electrical phone calls between places. They spent lots of money replacing burned out tubes. The search was on for something better.

20

Transistors Replace Tubes

The Bell Phone Company invented the transistor to replace vacuum tubes. The transistor is much smaller, uses less power and is more reliable.

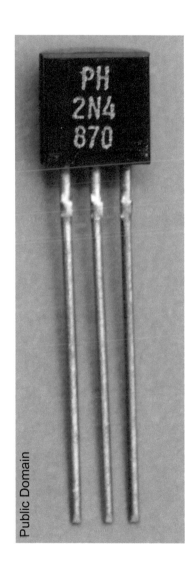

22

SAGE Keeps Bombers at Bay

In the 1950's Cold War, the USA was afraid that the USSR would attack them with planes carrying atomic bombs. The US spent over $10 Billion dollars on the SAGE System. This Computer-based Command and Control Network connected radar stations around the country and coordinated fighter aircraft and Air Defenses. Over a hundred sensors and computer centers were connected by long distance phone lines.

SAGE = Semi-Automatic Ground Environment

24

Missiles and Micro-Electronics

To overcome air defenses, both the US and USSR made intercontinental ballistic missiles that carried A-bombs. Computers needed to fit inside the missile. The push was on to make electronics smaller.

26

Space Race

The USSR and USA were each afraid that the other would put nuclear weapons into Space. Next, there was a Space Race to see who would get to the moon first.   Both sides used guidance computers and engines from their missiles on their moon rockets. In 1969, the USA was first to the moon. Today the USA uses Russian rockets to get to the space station.

28

Massive Mainframes

The design of nuclear missiles and Space Race rockets created demands for computers to do calculations. IBM created the 360 computer systems. The massive systems took a lot of people to set-up, program, run and maintain.

IBM noticed the mountains paper files that the military, businesses and universities used. IBM made huge and expensive mainframe computers to process all this data for anyone who could afford the millions of dollars that these systems cost.

30

Intel Invents Chips

Intel invented how to make thousands of transistors on a chip of silicon. Intel chips look like super highways of criss-crossing lines. Intel microchips are the computer's brains but brains alone do not a computer make.

Wikipedia

32

Hippies and Homebrew Computer Club

In the 1960's and 1970's , while IBM made mainframe computers, the Homebrew Computer Club was meeting at Stanford University. Their ideas were based on hippie counter-culture ideas. Their motto was to freely share information and make computers available to everyone.

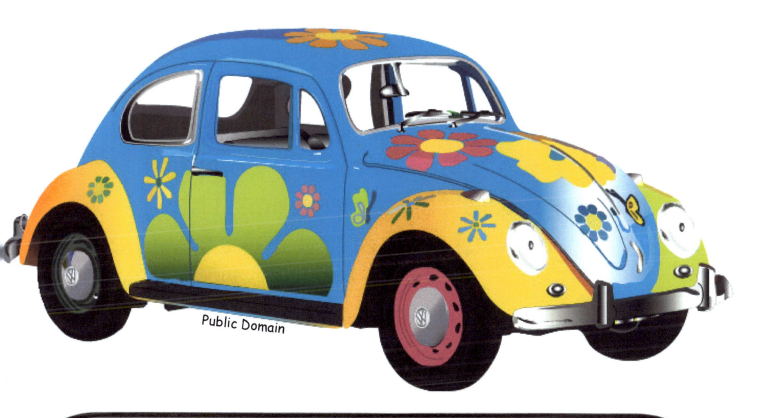
Public Domain

NEWSLETTER

Homebrew Computer Club

Robert Reiling, Editor ☐ Post Office Box 626, Mountain View, CA 94042 ☐ **Joel Miller**, Staff Writer

Typesetting, graphics and editorial services donated by **Laurel Publications**, 17235 Laurel Rd., Los Gatos, CA 95030 (408) 353-3609

Public Domain

Apples for All

Steve Jobs and his business partner Steve Wozniak created a company called Apple Computer Inc. They made computers personal & convenient.

35

Wikipedia by Ed Uthman

36

Alto is Ahead of its Time

In exchange for stock, Xerox let Steve Jobs and Apple engineers tour the Xerox research center called PARC. They saw a prototype of an office computer called Alto. It used a Graphical User Interface (GUI) and a mouse. Alto was very expensive.

38

Mac Makes it Easy

Steve Jobs leads Apple to create affordable Macintosh computers for home, office and school use. Its 'point and click' software was easy to use.
Results were printed on laser printers. The success of these computers led to competition.

Macintosh II

40

IBM PC and Clones

IBM made the Personal Computer, the PC, for home and office use.   Other companies started making PCs, called clones, as well.

42

The IBM PC used Microsoft operating system software. First DOS, then Windows.

File Edit Search Layout Mark Tools Font Graphics Help   (Press F3 for Help)

IN CONGRESS, JULY 4, 1776
The unanimous Declaration of the thirteen united States of
America

When in the Course of human events it becomes necessary for one
people to dissolve the political bands which have connected them
with another and to assume among the powers of the earth, the
separate and equal station to which the Laws of Nature and of
Nature's God entitle them, a decent respect to the opinions of
mankind requires that they should declare the causes which impel
them to the separation.

43

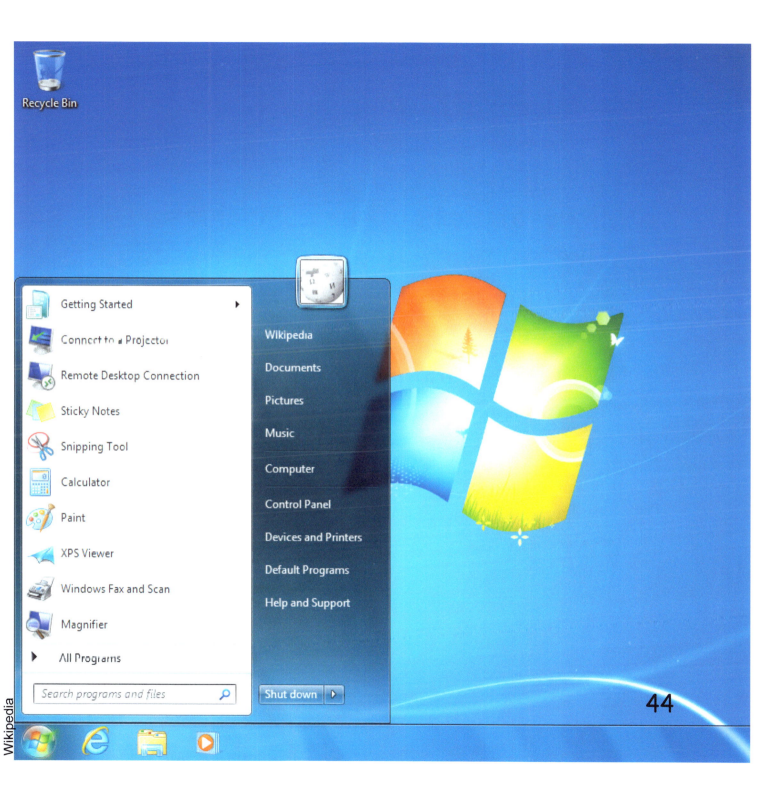

Microsoft-ware and More

Microsoft lets other companies make software applications based on Windows. This includes: word processors, spreadsheets and database managers etc.

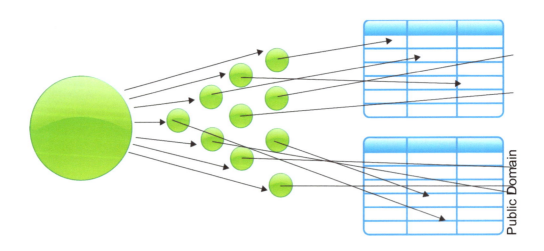

Public Domain

45

Column name

Formula

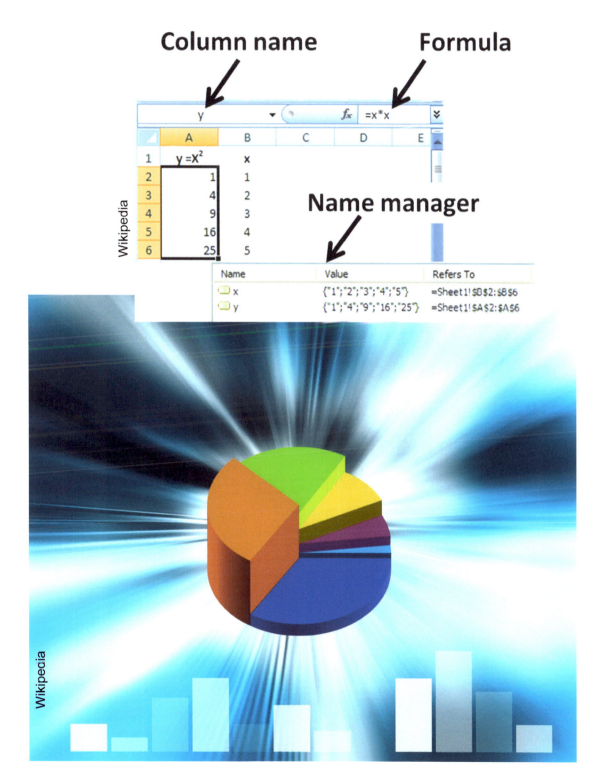

Name manager

y		f_x =x*x

	A	B	C	D	E
1	y =x²	x			
2	1	1			
3	4	2			
4	9	3			
5	16	4			
6	25	5			

Wikipedia

Name	Value	Refers To
x	{"1";"2";"3";"4";"5"}	=Sheet1!$B$2:$B$6
y	{"1";"4";"9";"16";"25"}	=Sheet1!$A$2:$A$6

Wikipedia

46

Super Cray's Big Day

The military and big businesses needed supercomputers to help design bigger atomic bombs or build better airplanes. In 1976, Supercomputer Cray-1 cost millions of dollars. It was the fastest computer of its time.

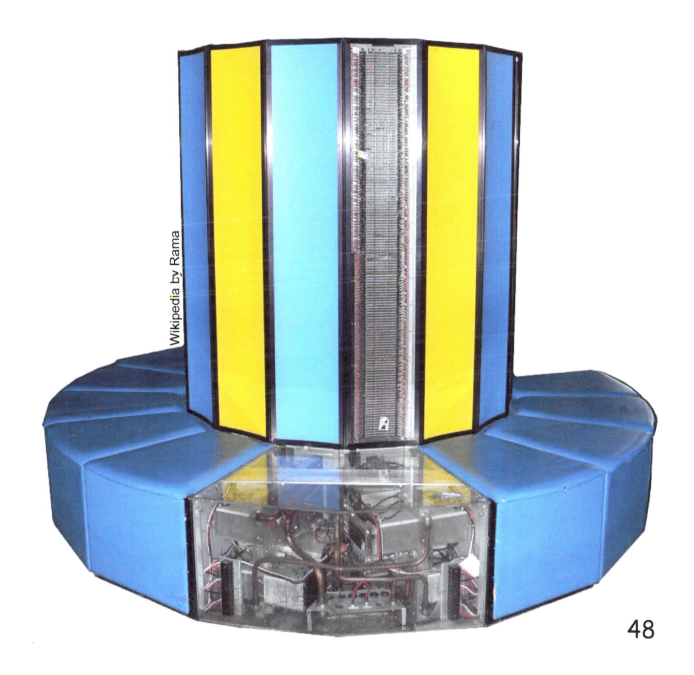

48

Intel's Integrated Insides

While supercomputers offered amazing computing capability to a few, Intel was busy adding more transistors and capabilities to their microprocessor chips.
In forty years, the number of transistor on a chip went from thousands to billions. All this in the space of a postage stamp. Chips are the electronic brains behind the computer revolution.

intel®

PCIset
SB82437VX
L6182051
SU085
INTEL Ⓜ © '95

LANs and WANs

Up to this point, it was all about making computers faster, smarter & cheaper. But something was missing.
Look at a microprocessor chip under a microscope. There are networks of interconnecting lines that are highways for data.

52

At first, a computer hooked up to peripherals like scanners and printers. Then, all the computers at one place were connected together into a local area network called a LAN.

Next, computers at different places were connected in a wide area network or WAN. Soon the web-like computer connections went worldwide. How did computer networks start?

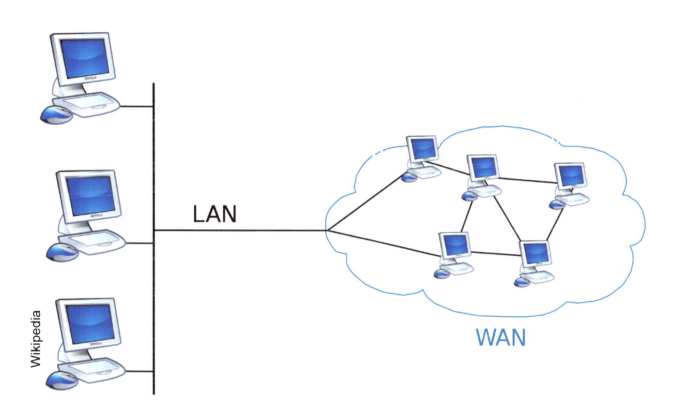

LAN

Wikipedia

WAN

54

ARPA-NET

Applying what was learned from the earlier SAGE program, the US Military funded connecting computers at Universities and Research Labs across the country. In the 1970's ARPANET pioneered critical network communication methods. For example, "packet switching" breaks down a message into parts. It sends the pieces by multiple telephone paths. At the destination, the pieces are put back together again.

Honolulu

Kjeller

MOFF
LBL
III
LINCOLN
MIT IPC
MIT MAC
CCA
BBN
BBN
RADC
SRI
UTAH
GWC
CASE
NCC
XEROX
CARNEGIE
HARVARD
HAWAII
AMES
AMES
TYMS
RUTGERS
STAN
PURDUE
ABERDEEN
NORSAR
FNWS
DOCB
ILL
URPAT
BELVOIR
UCL
USCB
SDAC
NBS
USDC
UCLA
MITRE
SDC
ARPA
RAND
AFWL
ETAC
USC
USC-I
RML

🟧 "TIP" - Kan tilknyttes
vertsmaskiner og terminaler

🔴 "IMP" Kan tilknyttes
vertsmaskiner

Wikipedia

56

NSF-NET

Starting in the 1980's, the
 National Science Foundation
or NSF made NSFNET to
promote general purpose
research. There were tens
of thousands of users. The
NSF developed a network
backbone. It is a way to
interconnect computer
networks together to share
scientific research data.

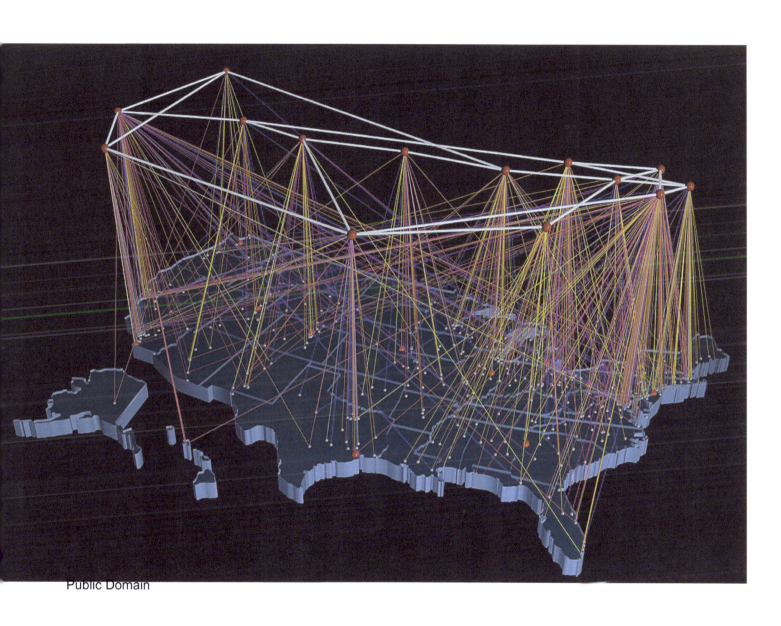

58

Internet Expands Exponentially

The NSFNET becomes the open Internet where anyone can join. Private companies run the commercial backbone but no one owns the Internet. It is the hardware and software that interconnects international networks of computers. Now that computers are connected, what can you do with them?

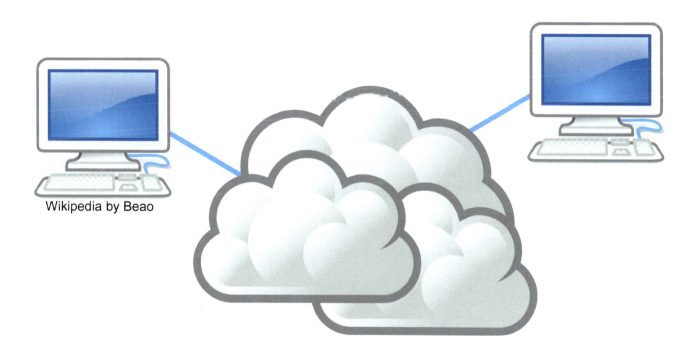

Wikipedia by Beao

60

Berners-Lee Keeps it Free

In the 1990's Tim Berners-Lee works for
CERN, a giant physics lab in Switzerland.
He notices how important documents
often get lost on-line.
He invents a way to link data so that
it is easy to store, retrieve and share.
He names his idea, the "World Wide Web."
At first it only works at CERN computers.
Tim freely shared his idea. Others
create ways for WWW to work on
different computer networks. Now, we
have browsers and search engines and
e-mail that interconnect the planet.

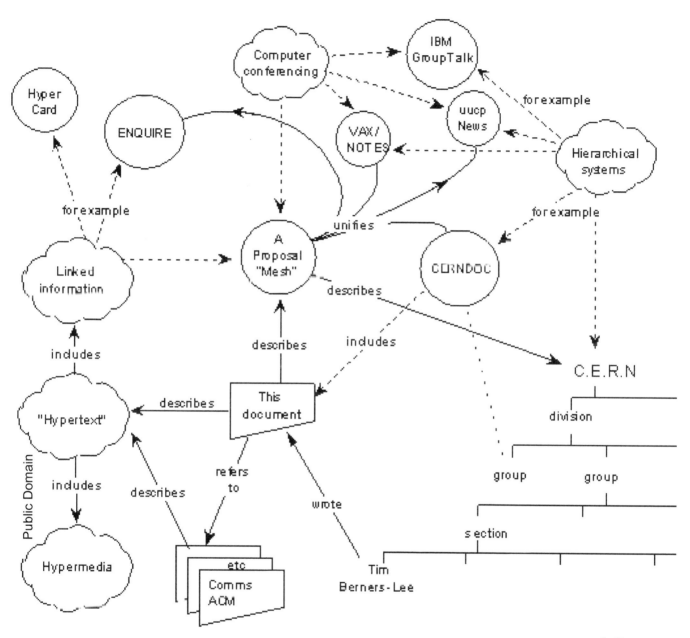

62

Today, over one-fourth of the people on the planet use the Internet and the World Wide Web.
That's over 2 Billion people on-line. Computers have come a long way from just counting people.

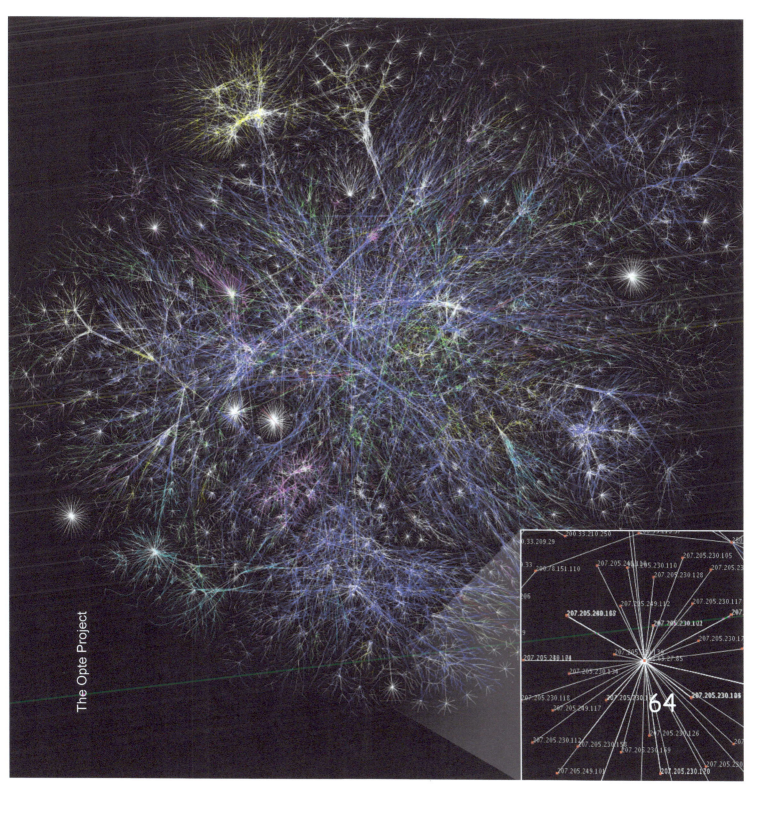

The Opte Project

200.33.210.250
200.33.209.29
200.78.151.110   207.205.244 205.230.110   207.205.230.105
207.205.230.128   207.205.23
207.205.249.112   207.205.230.117
207.205.240.163   207.205.230.101   207
207.205.230.17
207.205.230.104   207.205   27.85
207.205.230.134
207.205.230.118   207.205.230.119   64   207.205.230.10
207.205.249.117   207.205.230.126
207.205.230.112   207
207.205.230.158   207.205.230.159
207.205.249.101   207.205.230.120   207.205.230

Beyond the Roots of Real-Time

What are the roots of real-time computing? They are the creative expressions of the need to: count, compute and connect.

 Another word for connection is a nexus. Seeing where computers have come from, makes us wonder. Where will the next computer nexus lead?

66

Alford Books

www.alfordbooks.com

e-Books

available at:
www.alfordbooks.com

Printed Books

available at:
www.createspace.com
www.amazon.com

Buy Our Other Books:

All About England! - Worldwide Words
All About the USA! - The 50 State Quarters
All Are Equal - From Slavery to Civil Rights
Ant City - Mot and the Think Center
Art Intro - With Insects, Eggs & Oils
Bee's Sneeze - Overcome Obstacles
Big Die - Earth's Mass Extinctions
Brit Mu Briefly - From Seeds to Civilization
Catch Phrase Come-Froms - Origins of Idioms
Chase to Space - The Space Race Story
Civil Sense - What if There Wasn't a Civil War?
Common Come-Froms - Origins of Objects
Computer Come-Froms: The Roots of Real-Time
Computers Are Easy to Understand
Cozy Clozy - From Fibers to Fabrics
Different Words - Same Meaning
Easy English - Sounds, Signs & Sentences
Easy Science - 7 Eye Opening Ideas
Fishi and Birdy - A Fable of Friends
G Chicken & 5 K's - The Thai Alphabet
Hedgehogs Hug! - Many Ways to Show Love
Humi Bird - A Humble Tale
Images in Action - Why Movies Move
I's in US - Essence of America
Jungle Fire - Flee or Fix
Meaning of Money - The American Way
Money Math - With Funky Fairy
Monkey Star - Practice Before Play
Nature's Links of Life
Ogs, Zogs & Useful Cogs - A Tale of Teamwork
Panda Reads!
Queen Jeen - And The Thrown Throne
Robin's First Flight - Wings of Courage
Senses - From Sights to Smells
Shoe Walks - With Funky Fairy
Sky-Lings: An Intro to Airplanes
Space Maps: Trek to Mars
Stars of Days & Months - The Story of 7 & 12
Sun's Above the Clouds - A Sunny Point of View
Too Much TV - Undo, Too-Tain-Itis
Tree Trips - Wide Wonderful World
Turtle Jumps - A Tale of Determination
Where Cookies Come-From - From Dough to Delicious
Who Did What in World History? Past Echoes in the Present
Why is California Interesting? - Dreams of Gold
Why is Thailand Interesting? - Source of the Smiles
Yo Frog - The Surprising Songs

Please contact us at: info@alfordbooks.com or trythaiketco@gmail.com

Recommended further reading:

Computers
Are Easy to Understand

68

Douglas J. and Pakaket Alford

Acronyms

Acronym	Description
ARPA	Advanced Research Projects Agency
AT&T	American Telephone and Telegraph Company
CERN	European Organization for Nuclear Research
DOS	Disk Operating System
ENIAC	Electronic Numerical Integrator And Computer
GUI	Graphical User Interface
IBM	International Business Machines
IC	Integrated Circuit
Intel	Integrated Electronics Corporation
LAN	Local Area Network
NSF	National Science Foundation
PARC	Palo Alto Research Center
PC	Personal Computer
SAGE	Semi Automatic Ground Environment
USA	United States of America
USSR	Union of Soviet Socialist Republics
WAN	Wide Area Network
WWW	Worldwide Web

Credit

Research was performed at, but no endorsements are implied from the following:

. Computer History Museum
1401 N Shoreline Blvd.
Mountain View, CA 94043 USA
http://www.computerhistory.org/hours/

. Intel Museum
2200 Mission College Blvd,
Santa Clara, CA 95054 USA
http://www.intel.com/content/www/us/en/company-overview/intel-museum.htm

. Museum of Science & Industry
 Liverpool Rd, Manchester M3 4FP, United Kingdom
http://www.mosi.org.uk

. www.wikipedia.org

Learn Subjects, One Story at a Time!

Alford Books

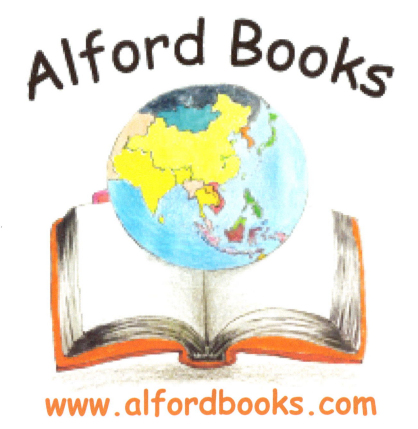

www.alfordbooks.com

www.ingramcontent.com/pod-product-compliance
Lightning Source LLC
Chambersburg PA
CBHW041421050326
40689CB00002B/603